MY PARANORMAL V.

MW01504576

First edition. November 1, 2024.

Copyright © 2024 BILL Simone.

ISBN: 979-8227445889

Written by BILL Simone.

Table of Contents

To my READER,

Bill Simmone

I would like to thank my daughter Angela Simone for editing this book, for her cover photo , and her photos inside this book. Angela's painting is on the cover of my second book, Contact From Beyond.

I want to thank my Daughter-N-Law Stephanie Simone for her support and encouragement then and now.

There Is a World I See

That Only Some Can Experience

My name is Bill Simone, my wife's name is Karen. I have two children, Bill Jr., and Angela. We have three terrific grandchildren; Isabella, Giavanna and Jennah.

Fourteen years ago, while I was still in my 60's, remarkable paranormal events started happening to me. I wrote down each experience in a journal format so I would not forget them. I am now sharing my journal because I want people to know about my experiences and to motivate others to share their paranormal experiences. Reading about my experiences with the paranormal will help you realize you are not alone. Yes, other people also have them. Keep in mind, as strange as your personal paranormal events may be, do not feel ashamed of your unexplained happenings. Believe in yourself and in your first-person experiences and share them with the world.

For as long as I can remember, my mother Ada would have paranormal experiences, and I have my mom on my mind when I write. As you read my journal entries, keep in mind that paranormal experiences come in varying forms and colors. Your paranormal experiences may or may not be like mine or anyone else's.

Bill Simone

MY PARANORMAL VISITS

A 14 YEAR JOURNEY

Volume 1

Chapter 1

The Years Between 2010 – 2012

My paranormal visits started fourteen years ago after moving into a new condominium complex. At first, I noticed a strong heat, heat sensation on my forearm, but not burning. It would happen at any location inside the condominium. Then, the shadow images started. When I mentioned it to my family, that is when they said I should start writing these events down. At this time, I did not realize some family members were also having their own experiences.

January 5th, 2010, Isabella came into the bedroom and asked me if we could talk, I responded "Yes, what would you like to talk about?" She said, "no one understands me like you do, Grandpa." I asked her again, "What do you want to talk about." She replied, "ghosts and souls." We talked about how our soul continues to live after death. I told her they no longer have a body like we do but they can move around as we do. Isabella was so excited about these friends that she told a friend at school about what was happening. Her friend at school started to talk about this.

February 6th, 2010, Isabella is now having conversations with her invisible friends on a regular basis (she is young and creative, so I encouraged her). She is always asking us for ideas on what she should talk about. We are always giving her ideas for her conversations. We tell her, ask them for a name, and what age they are. Ask if they have been with you for a long time. Ask what type of games they play. We asked Isabella a few days later, "were you able to talk with your friends?" Isabella replies "yes, they understand me, and I am happy."

April 11th, 2010, The family is having a party at my daughter-in-law's and son's house (Stephanie and Billy) and Isabella is 4 years old at that time. We are in the living room and dining room area that connects to the staircase leading upstairs. Isabella tells my son Billy that an angel had just gone up the stairs. Billy and Isabella dash upstairs hoping to see something. But nothing was seen.

On May 22nd, 2010, We moved in with my daughter and granddaughter, Angela, and Isabella, in the same condominium complex but a different unit. Angela twice saw a shadow figure appear to float across her room while Isabella was still talking with her imaginary friends, and I am still feeling the heat on my arms. Never a burn, or hot feeling, just warmth. I can compare it to walking past a stove or dishwasher when they are on and running. I look around and check to find a heat source, but nothing is on, not even the coffee maker. This will only last a couple minutes with every occurrence.

July 17th, 2010, One evening Karen and I were watching TV, and something caught my eye. From where I sat, I could see directly into the other room. I see the shadow figure Angela has occasionally caught through the corner of her eye. The figure looked like a square block for a body and two mountains on top. Mountain top ranges that are round on top, not peaked. You could not see through it. The figure seemed to pass through the walls, room to room. No sound and no provocation from the figure, negative or positive. Both Karen and I saw it.

Later that same evening, I had gotten up from my chair and walked across the room when I suddenly saw a dark, fully shaded figure walking slowly but at a natural walking pace. I watch it for a few seconds before I realize it is that shadow person Angela had described. As it comes out of the wall, it walks across the room and through the furniture, continuing through the furniture to the opposite wall. It never turns or investigates our room. It is a full shadow walking without any hesitation, just walking straight across the room. I cannot see through it, but it has a human form. What I saw had a more human shape than what Angela saw in her room.

July 19th, 2012, I will eventually see more shadow people in the future at various houses. These things now will happen over a two-year period while Karen and I are living with Angela and Isabella. Not knowing at this time in our lives different paranormal activities will follow Karen and I intermittently, during the next fourteen years.

CHAPTER 2

The Years Between 2014-2018

May 18th, 2014, we are now living at an apartment in the city of Eastlake. As I am sleeping on my recliner, I feel something touching my feet. Upon awakening and opening my eyes, I see the face of a young child, a girl, a child about three years in age. Just her face was visible and not clear. She had a blurry look, but this could be because I did not have my glasses on. She was facing me and all white like a misty cloud. From the shoulders down I could not see a body form. I also could not see the bottom of her because the leg of the recliner was up and covering a good portion of the body. I just had a feeling that there was not any form from the shoulders downward. She is just looking at me, no expression, no movement, just the look. After eight or ten seconds later the image slowly disappears, just slowly fading away.

May 21st, 2014, A few nights later, the little girl appears again. She does the same thing she did before and wakes me up by touching my feet. It startles me, and when I open my eyes, I can see it is a little girl looking at me with the face of a child. I had jerked upon waking; I make a noise. She also must have been startled by my noise because she started to move backwards and away from me immediately. As she is moving backwards, I call out to her, please do not go! Unfortunately, it did not stop her from fading away. This time she was fading at a faster pace. The next few nights I had convinced myself I would not make a noise or a sudden move and frighten her away. Unfortunately, she never appeared again.

June 15th, 2014, A few weeks have gone by, and Karen and I have not talked about the child that woke me up. One morning while Karen and I were having coffee, Karen asked me if I had walked into the bedroom the previous night and given her a kiss on her cheek. I said no, I had not. Karen said she was sure she was awakened by a kiss on her cheek. She made it clear it was not a dream, she felt a physical kiss familiar to a person. The kiss will occur a couple more times in the coming months.

October 12th, 2014, I am sitting in my chair listening to the radio, Karen starts walking into the living room and stops by the kitchen area to talk to me. As we are in the kitchen area (a small hallway that serves as an intersection between the kitchen, living room and dining room) talking, we hear something drop into the sink. Karen does see something out of the corner of her eye as it drops from underneath the cabinet. I do not see anything because there is a wall blocking my vision, but we both heard it drop. The sound of the drops is very loud, and it is easy to hear the distinct sound of something hitting the sink. As I say, "what the heck was that?" Karen is saying "something fell into the sink." Karen now says, "I just got a glimpse of something falling." I get up from the chair and we both walk into the kitchen and look in the sink. To our surprise, we do not see anything, not even a drop of water.

March 4th, 2015, I am sitting in my recliner around 1:00 AM, listening to the news on my radio with the ear plugs in. While I am listening, I am also playing a game on my phone, I am not asleep. While I am playing the game, something catches my attention from the corner of my eye. I realize it is the shadow of a person. The shadow is where the bedroom and hall join the living room. The shadow seems unsure if it should come into the living room. The shadow moves forward, backwards, and then starts turning in a circular motion. I started thinking it was Karen, so I said aloud, "What the hell are you doing Karen?" Then I wondered, has Karen started walking to the bathroom but changed her mind? The shadow then turns around and moves completely forward into the living room. I can see the shadow has the shape and hair style of an adult lady with a light-colored outline. The shadow does not move forward to me, instead, the shadow turns and moves straight to the wall that has a picture of two of my grandchildren, Isabella, and Giavanna. As I watch this shadow, I am still thinking the shadow is Karen going to look at the two pictures, so I say, "Karen, my God, if you are going to look at the pictures, let me turn the light on for you!" While I call out to Karen, I can still see the back of the shadow as it is looking at the pictures. I reach out to turn the light on the woman shadow disappears in that same instant. I did not see her fade away or disappear, she was just not there, gone. I start turning the light on and off hoping to see something, but I do not see anything indicating that anyone or anything was there. I can see it is just me alone and now mumbling to myself.

April 3rd, 2016, at 3:25 AM. I am awakened by a loud noise. I sat up at once trying to figure out what was happening. I quickly noticed the large 3x3 foot framed picture that was secured to the wall across from me had fallen. It is not a heavy picture, why did it fall? The two hooks are still in place and no tear on the back of the picture or on the wall. The picture has been hanging in that location for over a year without any problem. It had fallen straight down about six feet to the right of my chair.

May 26th, 2016, at 5:25 AM. I start getting up from my chair in the living room to wake Karen up in the bedroom. Today we are going out for breakfast with Jennah, Giavanna, and Isabella, and have a busy day ahead. As I entered the bedroom to wake Karen up, I heard a loud bang that seemed like it belonged to a heavy object that had suddenly fallen. "What was that, Karen?" She replies with, "I am not sure what it was, I was still waking up when it happened." I walked out into the living room and noticed my father's framed military flag had fallen from the wall where it was hanging. I notice the clock on the table is showing 5:25 AM. Exactly two hours from the time when the picture had fallen. The flag is in an enclosed shadow box with a wooden frame and glass. The shadow box is heavy and was securely hanging on the wall. It landed just at the edge of the table away from the lamp, clock, Kleenex box, and my cell phone. It did not fall straight down but about two feet forward from the wall and never hit anything. As if it was placed at the edge of the table facing outwards.

In a separate experience but around the same period as when the framed flag fell, Karen is kissed again, and we both continue to see shadows and a mist. This is the last time Karen will feel the kiss at night. The appearance of the mist is now increasing. Also, during this time I am continuously feeling the sensation of heat on my arms. As if I am walking past the dishwasher, oven, or coffee maker. But they are not on, and I am not in the kitchen.

Thursday, September 1st, 2016. Karen and I decided to move again, to the same city, a different building. Activity begins within a week of our arrival. Our new unit is in front of the building and next to the front entrance, so we can see and hear some nearby foot traffic regularly. Karen and I heard the apartment buzzer (there is a central buzzing system to get into the building as in most apartments), so we buzzed back right away to let them in, and we realized no one was there. This happens every day, sometimes more than once during the day, for a two-week period. Karen and I are starting to think that kids in the neighborhood are playing a joke on us. We have a slide-door that opens from the living room out to our private cement patio. From there, you can easily walk a few feet to the entrance doors and central buzzing system. There are only a few privacy bushes between our patio and the entrance. Karen and I decided to keep the glass slider open, and the screen unlocked so we would be able to get outside immediately to catch them if we continue to get pranked. We were not able to see anyone by the door or the entrance area of the apartment. We called maintenance to let them know that there is a malfunction with the apartment buzzer. We began asking our neighbors if they had any experiences like this. We wanted to know before maintenance came the next day. All the residents we spoke with have said no. Karen and I asked the neighbors if the previous tenants shared similar experiences with the buzzer. Their response was the same, nothing was ever mentioned.

Later in the day, maintenance is here pressing the buttons on the buzzer system to problem solve, and everything is working fine. Their answer was it must be the weather, and they had never heard of such a thing like this ever happening. I have a problem with the weather being the cause because it has been very dry for the past few weeks.

Once every day for two days the buzzer goes off and no one is there. That was the last occurrence.

Chapter 3

New Activity and Events

It is somewhere in Mid-January 2019 (not sure of date). As I start to wake up, I notice there are dark lines in my visual field. These lines are in the shape of a square. I think I must have been rubbing my eyes and did not notice, and this was the cause. I then intentionally rub my eyes while continuing to look at the lines for about ten to fifteen seconds. This has now happened a couple of times a week. I tell Karen that I might be starting to have paranormal experiences again and explain to her what I have been seeing. My daughter-in-law Stephanie is a believer of personal paranormal experiences, so I reach out to her with this update. Stephanie encourages me to write these events down. I say I have been writing some but not in detail. Stephanie insists that I start writing in more detail, so I do.

The occurrence of these paranormal lines has started to increase as well as the clarity of the lines themselves. These lines are very pronounced and easy to see. I am sure that this time I am not rubbing my eyes as I wake up. What is this energy provoking me to wake up if it is energy?

March 9th, 2019, at 7:40 PM. I wake up from sleeping, no lights are on except for a small nightlight to my side. As I continue to wake, I notice a dark, solid line in my visual field in the shape of a square with pulsating lights moving juxtapositioned to the square. The moving lines are very thin but move rapidly along the outline of the square. The juxtapositioned lines change from pulsating to a zig-zag formation along the square. The moving lines can be compared to electromagnetic waveforms. The entire occurrence lasts around one minute.

March 15th, 2019, at 9:45 PM. I am awoken from sleep by a physical nudge familiar to a person's touch. In my visual field there is a rectangular shape made of dark lines that move back and forth from vertical and horizontal. It has the same type of light movement along the box line. The only light on in the room is my usual small nightlight to the side.

March 16th, 2019, at 8:30 PM. I am awoken again from sleep by a physical touch familiar to a person's touch as the night before. I see the same dark lines as the nights before but instead of a rectangle, there are three vertical squares with a juxtapositioned white light moving very slowly along the squares. The white lights still remind me of electromagnetic waveforms.

March 18th, 2019, at 11:10 PM. I am again awakened from a firm touch on the front part of my leg, just above my kneecap. I see the three vertical squares made of dark lines about a foot away from my face. I let out a noise of exclamation and surprise as I simultaneously move my head back and away from the squares, they slowly fade away and disappear. This event will occur on a regular basis during the next couple of weeks, but not close to my face, it will be about six feet away.

April 2nd, 2019, at 9:35 PM. I am awakened by a very firm nudge on the front of both legs around the knee area. The lines of the square are dark and solid with visibly different energetic activity moving around it. That single square begins to morph into three connected squares each with a visibly distinct energy moving around the shape. The juxtapositioned energy is white, red and the third I cannot make out (I have color blindness). The squares are making exceedingly small fluctuations forwards and backwards as they rotate. The squares remain connected as they begin to change their form into a shape I do not recognize. I ask aloud, "if you are trying to show me something, you have to come closer." They pause for a few seconds, and then the connected squares slowly start moving towards me as it clarifies. Astonished, I put my glasses on! The movement towards me gets faster, and I can see it even clearer. It is three very distinct old gravestones with rounded tops and unclear writing on the front of each gravestone. I am shocked by the images, and I say loudly, "Oh my God, they are gravestones!" Simultaneously, the squares move away from me as they fade to gone. The images of the gravestones were never seen again, but the pulsating energy lines will continue.

Chapter 4

New Images

Saturday April 13th, 2019, at 10:30 PM. I woke up alarmed by a hard physical nudge on the front of my leg around my knee. What or who has just touched me? My eyes open to a straight, stationary vertical line about six feet in front of me. Juxtaposed to the vertical line is a separate and wavy energy line that is small and narrow and moves slowly. The wave is like an oscilloscope and does not pulsate. The entire image lasts about fifteen to twenty seconds and then just vanishes in an instant without fading. The only light on is the bedroom nightlight. This is the first image seen since the three gravestones.

Monday April 15th, 2019, at 10:05 PM. I am forcefully, nearly pushed awake. As I open my eyes, I again clearly see the vertical line. The line is clear and about one foot in length. The line is about one foot and stationery and juxtapositioned to the vertical line is a separate line of energetic activity moving vertically and flashing lightly along the stationary line. The secondary line of movement stays within the length of the stationary vertical line.

Tuesday May 7th, 2019, at 7:30 PM. I was awakened from something touching my leg. As I opened my eyes, I noticed a small light orange and yellow orb moving very rapidly away from me as it faded.

Tuesday May 14th, 2019, at 8:20 PM. When I sleep in my recliner, I leave the nightlight on by my side. I feel a nudge like before, not once, but twice. Initially, as I open my eyes, I do not see anything. As I start looking around the room, I suddenly notice to my left, two, faint blue orbs the size of baseballs, alongside each other circling in a clockwise direction (five feet up from the floor in the center of the wall). After a few seconds, the left orb begins to move counterclockwise as the right one continues clockwise as they remain alongside each other. The one orb moves away from me and disappears into the left side of the wall and then the other through the right side of the wall.

Thursday May 30th, 2019, at 8:27 PM. I wake up to a firm touch on my leg and see four, slightly wavy, dark lines, equal in length, moving slowly upward towards and through the ceiling. The activity lasts about five seconds before they disappear.

Sunday *June 2nd, 2019, at 8:35 PM.* I fell asleep in the recliner with my pajamas on and a blanket over me. I awake to more than the previous touch or a nudge! I feel a firm push down on my left leg a few inches below the knee and open my eyes to a group of small circles grouped together, like the blowing soap bubbles through a wand as a kid. The circles are about the size of baseballs and are all intertwined with each other with the activity occurring in and contained in a circumference of about two feet. Each circle has a separate and distinct, wavy, line of activity that is juxtapositioned to the orbs moving in smooth, spiral patterns, that are yellowish orange. The orbs smoothly and simultaneously move around each other while the secondary lines remain attached until eventually the entire visualization fades away through the ceiling. I am astonished. *Second event of the same evening.* I reached for my knee after being awoken by a firm nudge on the leg. My eyes open to see the same group of circles! The circles are transparent, not solid. The circles are the same size, moving with the same motions and limited to the same circumference in the upper corner of the wall. The same secondary energy line is present with a faint pulse and remarkably close to the primary lines of the circles. The circles fade away as they go upwards through the ceiling. The event lasts around 90 seconds (about 1 and a half minutes), I confirm the time just as the activity ends.

Friday June 7th, 2019th, at 8:42 PM. I am awakened from a sound sleep in my recliner to a light touch on my abdomen. While opening my eyes I can see that group of circles again. Their size and shapes are exactly what I have seen before. This time though there is a difference, the group of circles are moving fast in an upward direction toward the ceiling. Same size circles, the group was about two feet by two feet in circumference. I could see the outline of each circle, the movement of flashing light around each one. Each circle was not solid but transparent. As they reach the ceiling the entire group fades away while going through the ceiling. All the circles kept their form, being clear in the center and perfectly round.

Wednesday June 12th, 2019, at 9:43 PM. I am firmly nudged on the lower part of my left leg. I was reading a book in the living room with the light on (60-watt bulb with a white shade) behind me. I look up to my left, about two feet up I see six to eight circles intertwined together slowly moving upward. The room-darkening curtain is pulled shut in the living room, so I immediately rule out the possibility of seeing car lights. I do not have any light or glare entering the room. I am awake with my eyes open and clearly see the circles in the room. I hold my gaze at the circles to confirm the primary lines of the circles are identical to the previous events occurring this month, but without any visible secondary energy movement. The group of circles remain intertwined as they move upwards towards the ceiling and fade away.

Thursday June 13th, 2019, at 8:46 PM. I wake up naturally, and without any nudge that I notice. As I open my eyes, I am startled by four vertical lines about six inches away from my face. I shouted out "what the hell" being surprised and flabbergasted! There were no additional movements like flashing, moving up, down or sideways. The event lasts about five seconds before it just vanishes, similarly, to turning the light on and off, just gone in an instant.

Friday June 21st, 2019, at 9:35 I woke up from sleep to a nudge on my right arm, and I see the same number of circles (six to eight circles ten feet in front of me, and six feet up from the floor). I clearly see each circle having a secondary line (like an electrical charge). There are no colors to note during this event. After thirty seconds the circles start to move away from me and slowly fade.

Sunday June 23rd, 2019, at 7:15 PM. I am awakened without a nudge and see the same group of circles but fewer, stationery, and not with the same clarity. Without notice, the group moves sideways (to my right) and disappears before reaching the wall. This event in total lasts about fifteen seconds.

Tuesday July 2nd, 2019, at 10:20 PM. It is happening again. A firm nudge just above my left knee wakes me up and I see there are two separate groups of intertwined circles, about six feet up from the floor and three feet apart from each other. Each group has five baseball size circles, each circle made of a primary dark line with a separate secondary line that appears to move around the primary line familiar to a pulsating motion. Neither group had movement restricted nor confined to a certain circumference, like past events. The two groups of circles move around each other in a circular pattern familiar to a group of bugs around a streetlight at night. The event in total lasts about sixty seconds or slightly longer when the two groups move rapidly in different directions and disappear.

Chapter 5

Different Images and Happenings

Sunday July 14th, 2019, at 11:31 PM. Another push or nudge woke me up from slumber in my recliner, and I immediately start looking around the room to see nothing. I continued a few seconds of eagerly searching for the room as a sudden flash of light demanded my attention from the kitchen. I remained in my recliner (the same recliner in the same place in the same room) and saw a shadow moving through the kitchen nightlight and thought to myself, it must be Karen up to a drink (we keep the nightlight on in the kitchen to avoid turning on the main ceiling light). My gaze fixed towards the kitchen, the nightlight went dim and then back to normal brightness. Having seen the shadow cross the nightlight, I say aloud, "Are you in the kitchen, Karen?" No response from her.

I wonder what is going on and I think to myself; I am awake and not half asleep; I know I saw these things happening. I look again around the room sure something is there. Nothing. As I turn towards the kitchen, a bright yellow or orange orb reveals itself and slowly makes jerking movements around the fuse box and starts moving down toward the dishwasher (below the fuse box). The orb gives me a feeling it is looking at everything with curiosity. The shadow (the shadow exists separately but simultaneously to the orb in the room) moves above the kitchen countertop and starts elongating from a softball size and shape to oval (or a loaf of bread) approximately one and a half feet long and narrow with a vibrating motion.

The event continued uninterrupted for five minutes, so I thought it was safe to start slowly reaching for my glasses to confirm this event. The orb is a bright yellowish color with an orange tint at the same height as the fuse box but has changed location and is now at the folding door of the pantry.

After seven minutes of continuous activity, I decided I was going into the kitchen to further investigate. I briefly take my eyes off the orb to stumble into my slippers and lose sight of the orb. As I walk into the kitchen there is no physical or visual sign of an orb or anything else out of the ordinary, including the nightlight on as usual.

The next morning, I asked Karen if she had heard me call out her name. She replied, "I did not hear anything, I slept soundly the entire night."

Friday July 19th, 2019, at 7:58 PM. I am sleeping in the usual recliner with only the night light on behind me. As I wake from a touch on my leg, I see a group of intertwined of eight to ten, baseball sized, transparent circles. Each circle is made of a stationary solid dark line with a flashing secondary line that is twisting around each individual circle. The circles remain stationary as I visualize the group for only a few seconds, and then they instantly disappear.

Monday July 23rd, 2019, at 10:00 PM. I am reading an article on my cell phone with the lamp on at the end table next to me making the room bright. Something catches my eye about three feet in front of me and a foot off the ground. I clearly and easily start observing three circles intertwined together and very slowly moving upwards to disappear through the ceiling. No flashes, secondary movements or colors observed. This event reminded me of blowing bubbles out of a wand when you were a kid and watching the bubbles slowly flowing away and disappearing.

Friday July 25th, 2019, at 3:00 PM. I fell asleep in the recliner in the living room facing the sliding patio doors, as usual. I am not sure if I was nudged, poked, or if a noise woke me up, but something does. As I start to wake up, I see a spider hanging mid-air from the web. I realize what I am observing resembles a pair of cat eyes of two varied sizes! The eyes are in front of me and to the right of the chair (both the pair of cat eyes and I are facing the same direction. However, I am currently looking at the cat eyes as the cat eyes maintain their gaze outside of the patio windows). I intentionally moved my gaze down and right towards the nightstand, and into the lenses of my glasses to see the reflection of the cat's eyes. I cannot discern whether I was witnessing a second pair of eyes in my glasses, or if I was witnessing a reflection of the eyes I had already identified in midair.

Next, I reach for my glasses and put them on regardless of what I see. I see the cat's eyes, midair, I realize that the 'midair cat eyes' must have repositioned and are now very clearly looking directly at me. Frightened, I raise my arms to swing at the 'midair eyes' and knock them down and away. Instead, the eyes start moving towards me and get remarkably close to my face as I simultaneously start to hear a tapping or knocking at the sliding patio doors (originating from inside the Livingroom, not from outside on the patio that abruptly). I think to myself, could

I hit the cat eyes when I was swinging at them with my arms, and now the knocking sounds are complaints? The knocking sound stops abruptly along with my visualization of the cat eyes.

I thought for a little while about what happened until I fell back to sleep.

Friday July 26th, 2019, at 3:00 PM. Karen and I are talking in the living room, and a quick flash catches my eye down the hall. I slightly turn my head in that direction, and out of the corner of my eye I see the back of a girl's head quickly moving down the hall. She has three braids hanging from the back of her head that seem to end just above her shoulder blades. She remains in my vision as she moves further down the hall, but her energy starts turning into a misty light gray look. The outline of her body slowly fades away before reaching the end of the hall.

July 26th, 2019, at 9:30 PM. (Second event on July 26.) Karen is watching TV in the main bedroom as I am sleeping in the spare bedroom (we use this room for sleep, computer work, and leisure). While lying on her side watching TV, Karen notices a shadow of a man wearing a hat. She tells me it was a pirate-type hat with three pointed tips. The shadow man was gray, with a complete side form, wearing a hat touching the ceiling, indicating just how high from the floor the figure is. Now proceeds very slowly across the room and through the wall. It never stops to glance at her or turns looking in her direction. Karen later says, "I had the feeling he didn't even realize that I was there." Where it went after going through the wall we do not know.

Saturday August 10th, 2019, at 1:35 – 2:05 AM. I feel a strong push on my legs that wakes me up. I walked around only to notice the bedroom and kitchen nightlights were on, everything seemed normal. I got back into my chair and was surprised by the nightlight on in the kitchen, dimming then getting brighter, over, and over. I continued to sit in my chair for a few seconds staring into the kitchen to observe. I realize I am witnessing two separate orbs, the size of golf balls, moving in a circular motion around each other, like bugs at a streetlight. One is yellow and the second one a light red color. I put on my glasses to confirm what I was witnessing. Yes, two orbs are moving in the kitchen about a foot below the ceiling and close to the wall, continuing to move like moths around a streetlight at night. I briefly watched with amazement.

I say aloud directly to the orbs, "can I help you; would you like to talk?" Both orbs stopped moving at the sound of my voice without any change in color and grew to the size of a baseball while remaining a foot below the ceiling, and a foot away from the kitchen wall. I say again in a more forceful tone with clear questioning, "can I do anything for you; would you like to talk?" Only the yellow orb begins to move slowly towards me. I think to myself, oh no, what happened to the red orb? I last remember seeing the red orb near the fuse box.

The yellow orb moves down to the edge of the counter then quickly upwards toward the fuse box and shrinks in size. I say directly, "I want to talk with you, and help you." For the second time it moves towards me, faster and faster, then suddenly stops in the hallway as the yellow orb grows bigger to the size of a softball, and brighter, and now some orange in the center (reminder, I am colorblind.) The entire orb is transparent, with a darker center that fades at the edges. I immediately check to confirm my glasses are on, they are. I say, "I don't know what you want me to do; is there any way I can help you?" I am estimating a few minutes passed with the orb at the doorway and me trying to communicate with it.

Now the orb begins moving backwards about two feet away from me while enlarging in size, without any noticeable change in color. I see the orb float near the fuse box and vanish in an instant. The red orb was not again observed.

Saturday August 10th, 2019, at 2:15 AM. (Second event of the day) I spent about 30 minutes in my chair watching the clock tick and reflecting on what I had just witnessed. I got up only to wake Karen and tell her what happened. I nudged, poked, and pushed, but she did not wake up. Karen was so sound asleep she did not even complain to me in her sleep. I go back into the bedroom and get in the recliner and just stare into the kitchen in disbelief.

Disbelief soon manifests into a reality as I notice the single yellow orb has returned in the kitchen. I call out directly to the single orb as I had before while sitting up and leaning forward, "what can I help you with; can we talk about anything?" I am not getting a response; is the orb ignoring me deliberately? I do not observe a change in size or color. I lay back in the recliner, pulled the covers over me, and watched the activity in kitchen for about fifteen minutes until I fell asleep unbothered.

Friday August 16th, 2019, at 8:50 PM. I am reclined in my chair asleep when I am awakened by a solid nudge on my leg. I open my eyes to see the group of circles have returned! I clearly observe five circles, each the size of a golf ball with a transparent center. The group of circles are not intertwined with each other however they are connected at multiple points along their individual perimeters, but not linked like a chain. The lights were pulsating as a single unit as if I were looking at an electric signal of an oscilloscope. I observe the activity for about thirty seconds before the group slowly fades away from me.

Sunday August 18th, 2019, at 8:20 PM. Today is my birthday and the entire family attended my party. This party was a terrific surprise, and I give credit to my daughter-in-law, Stephanie, who organized it at the last minute.

I came home and fell asleep in my chair with my table lamp on a foot behind me to my right (it has a sixty-watt bulb, so I have sufficient lighting in the room). I had been reading on my cell phone when I fell asleep with the light on. I woke up briefly and quickly reached for the light and turned it off. Immediately afterwards, as I am lowering my arm down and away from the switch, I feel a noticeably light nudge on my abdomen. As I felt this, I quickly reached forward to turn the light back on and I lifted my eyes to observe three stationary curved lines, about three feet in front of me. I briefly observe the lines as they rapidly disappeared. This is a strange way to end the day.

Sunday August 18th, at 10:03 PM. (Second event of the day.) I felt a push on my leg just above the knee and opened my eyes to see two of the three lines from earlier in the evening. Both lines were curved and stationary for about five seconds before moving backwards to disappear.

Wednesday August 21st, 2019, at 10:09 PM. My lamp is on my side table illuminating the room, I fell asleep with it on. I woke up from a hard nudge on my leg and saw two lines about one foot away from my face.

I let out a noise of surprise but maintained my focus on the two vertical lines moving upward and through the ceiling. I watch for a few seconds when I am nudged again on my leg. I look down at my leg and do not see anything, so I look hastily back up to see one vertical line moving upwards, as if through the ceiling, to disappear. There were only a few seconds between each nudge.

Saturday August 24th, 2019, at 8:35 PM. As I am falling asleep in my recliner, I wake to it shaking and rocking. Suddenly, I felt something grab my elbow! Wide-eyed, I look down to see a rectangular shape the size of an envelope; brownish, greenish, and opaque. The shape is so close I yelp aloud and start calling across the apartment for Karen who enters the room about thirty seconds later, but the image is gone.

Monday August 26th, 2019, at 8:20 PM. While in the recliner feeling comfortable and sleepy I notice; one, small, straight, vertical line to my right, about the height of the back of the chair I am in. Karen walks into the room and startles me fully awake. I looked around the room, but the lines were gone.

Monday August 26th, 2019, at 10:17 PM. (Second event, same night.) I stayed awake from the earlier episode this evening to listen to the radio with my earbuds in, so I do not disturb Karen. I noticed the same small line to my right at the height of the recliner. I quickly think it through in my head; I have not felt anything, the light is on, the image is clear and not a reflection or a glare from anything in the room. The line slowly floats towards me until it is two feet in front of my face. I became astonished and curious. I clearly discern the line is horizontal formation with the ends more prominent. The middle of the lines is constructed of opaque dots the size of a BB pellet. There is a curved line dangling from the left end I said, "what would you like to talk about?" I received no response. I watched while it moved upward towards the ceiling, gradually fading, and disappearing.

Tuesday August 27th, 2019, at 8:52 PM. I wake up and immediately see the small line that crossed my face last night (August 26, 2019). There are some differences; the line is vertical and flickering (like Christmas lights) with a solid curve on top and bottom without the dotted center or an associated color. Simultaneously, the image is moving upwards and seems to fade while passing through the ceiling.

Thursday August 29th, 2019, at 9:05 PM. While watching a football game on TV, I feel the pressure of the repeated nudge on my knee. With an automatic reflex, I turn my head to see the same small line from the previous nights. This one is a bit smaller without colors or flashing lights. The observation was brief and ended quickly.

Saturday August 31st, 2019, at 8:15 PM. I am simultaneously nudged on both knees. As I wake, I see three lines about one foot in length. The two outer lines are solid and straight while the three center lines are curved and intertwined. My observation lasts ten seconds before the lines disappear in midair.

Wednesday September 4th, 2019, at 8:40 PM. I woke up from sleeping without a nudge and see five feet in front of me a group of circles the size of golf balls contained within a square circumference of one foot by one foot. The circles are not intertwined but touch each other along their perimeter. There was not any flashing or colors around the circles. The circles move upwards and disappear before hitting the ceiling. I never felt a nudge, why did I wake up?

Thursday September 12th, 2019, at 9:15 PM. I feel a nudge on my side that wakes me up to see three stationary vertical lines for two minutes before they quickly fade away.

September 24th, 2019, at 8:45, September 24th, 2019, at 10:30 PM and September 25th, 2019, at 1:20 AM. I woke up surprised three separate times to feel unusually firm pushes against both of my legs near the knee.

I did not see any; lines, circles, flashing colors or pulsating activity. Even the room remained ordinary and unchanged. This was a triple event; two observations at night and one the next day early in the morning.

Friday September 27th, 2019, at 9:35 PM. This vision is slightly different. I wake to see three curved lines to my left, and three curved lines to my right. The lines are about a foot long and pulsating and observed for only fifteen seconds before quickly vanishing, as if a light switch turned the lines off.

Saturday September 28th, 2019, at 10:00 PM. As I am reading there is a light on to my right and slightly behind me. The room darkens enough to get my attention. I look up and around and I do not observe anything unusual. The light then seems to return to its original brightness. After thinking about it, I questioned if something had crossed in front of the light creating a 3 second shadow. I got up to investigate but I did not find the cause.

Monday September 30th, 2019, at 9:45 PM. I am reading in my chair as usual with both the lamp and night light on when I noticed a change in the brightness of the overall room. I quickly turned to look behind me to clearly see one dark circle, the size of a basketball, moving away from the light. As the room returns to its original brightness the circle is floating close to the floor, moving along the baseboard on its way to the closet doors to disappear from my vision at the closet.

Wednesday October 2nd, 2019, at 9:45 PM. I am listening to the radio when I feel something touching the top of my head. I brushed my head with my hand and expected to find a spider crawling on me, so I glanced for one to fall, without any luck. I look upward to see a group of vertical lines moving rapidly away from me! I quickly grabbed my glasses to confirm the details. Although they did not leave the room, I feared they were on their way out. For now, they stayed clearly visible and stationary, about six feet away from me, as if they were curious to communicate. I say aloud and directly, "can I help you?" Without a response, I intentionally get up and walk to the lines.

As I approach the four vertical lines, I am confirming several details; they are a flashing, mixture of; blue, orange, red, and a touch of yellow (with my color blindness, I cannot be positive with the color). As I stand only foot away, I ask, "how can I help?" and immediately start moving my hand slowly underneath the lines. The bottom of the lines are two feet from the floor, so I do not have to raise my hand to get underneath them.

The lines begin to move slowly away from me as a group, so loudly plea, "wait, don't go," provoking the lines further away and upwards while they very slowly fade away. I turn around to look at the clock, "I don't believe it!" Fifteen minutes had gone by, but it only felt like a minute.

Friday October 12th, 2019, at 11:05 PM. As Karen was walking towards the kitchen, she noticed a dark shadow, in the form of a human in the kitchen, that vanished ten seconds later.

Wednesday October 16th, 2019, at 1:00 AM. I am in my chair with my eyes closed, not sleeping, just thinking, relaxing. I notice through my closed eyelids a change of brightness in the room. I open my eyes to see the overall light in the room seems a little darker. Furthermore, I noticed the small area in front of the nightlight was getting darker, then returning to normal brightness. I discerned by observation the bulb is not flashing or dimming in any way, this change is only happening in front of the light, and I could now also see something floating around it. I got out of the chair and approached something floating familiar to fog or mist. Suddenly, it was gone, and the light in the room was normal again! I circled back to the recliner just as the activity resumed, so I quietly observed it for about five minutes before it stopped.

October 20th, 2019, at 4:20 PM. As I sleep in my recliner in the living room, TV on and blinds open, I wake from a firm nudge on my leg.

I look around the room, but I do not observe any activity. Karen was watching TV around the corner in the main bedroom. I told her what had happened, but she did not notice anything unusual.

October 21st, 2019, at 9:005 PM. I wake up from a nudge on both my legs and immediately start looking for the circles and lines. I scanned the room to see the lights and TV were on in the main bedroom, otherwise nothing unusual. I later asked Karen if she had anything unusual happen to her, she had not.

Wednesday October 23rd, 2019, at 10:49 PM. I feel a strong push downward on my left leg through the blankets. I open my eyes to see an orb about one foot in front of my face and six inches upwards, suspended in midair (I must look slightly upwards for a clear view). Both of my arms and hands remain tucked underneath the blanket, yet I can feel the orb putting pressure on the back of only my right hand. Slowly, I lift my hand from underneath the blanket while maintaining my gaze and concentrating on the orb. During those brief moments, I am clear that I can see the orb and it is not making physical contact with the blanket. As I continue to withdrawal my hand, the pressure stops. I again address the orb, "can I help you in some way; are you able to give me a signal that I will be able to understand?" as it begins moving away from me to fade. I am going to estimate that one minute has passed in total. I reached for my cell phone on the nightstand, I desperately wanted a picture of this, but as I turned back around to face the orb, it was gone.

Frantically, I start taking pictures everywhere I can; towards the ceiling, floor, and walls. I do

not want to miss any area of the room. I do not know if the orb is still present, but it is not

visible to my eye. I stopped to review all the pictures that I had taken, nineteen in total. I talk to myself with disappointment, damn, I did not get a picture of the orb. After sifting thought all

the photos, I realized I did capture the orb at picture seventeen (of nineteen)! I spent a few

minutes analyzing; the orb is in a blurred, zig zag pattern of movement, of the same colors I

observed in the past. The room looks like this; just the nightlight is on; across from me are the

patio doors dressed in a single, solid, room darkening curtain, without additional ambient light

getting into the room. The same effect as with a bug, a streak of an object while it is flying

extremely fast past you. saw in the kitchen while talking to them. But they were clearer than

what I captured with the cell camera and had the cell picture blown up to a 3x5 photo.

Saturday October 26th, 2019, at 2:40 AM. As I am going down the hall towards the dining room, I see a shadow. I investigated the living room and kitchen, realizing the shadow had returned. I observe the shadow moving towards the bedroom wall. I confirm there are no outside lights coming through the windows. I look towards the shadow and see it moving in a zigzag pattern upwards, to the dark side of the room. The shadow form blends with the darkness in the upper corner of the room until I can no longer see it.

MY PARANORMAL VISITS A 14 YEAR JOURNEY

Monday October 28th, 2019, at 8:44 PM. While I am resting with my eyes closed, thinking about how fast my three grandchildren; Isabella, Giavanna, and Jennah are growing up, when something hits my right knee. My body jerks as my eyes burst open to see; a group of tangled lines in crisscrossing pattern about three feet from the floor, without color or additional movements, and restricted to a circular circumference by only a single line. Only the single line looks like an oscilloscope. The group of lines faded within one minute from the start of observation.

Tuesday October 29th, 2019, at 2:20 AM. I am awake and reading the news headlines on my cell phone with the usual light on when I hear an unfamiliar voice of a child. I am not sure, but it sounds as if it is saying, Ma. I heard the voice again, and about three minutes later it said mom. It sounds as if the words came from the front room or kitchen area. We do not have any children in any of our eight adjoining units. The residents also do not have any grandchildren in the building for a voice to carry, as well it is quite early in the morning.

Thursday October 31st, 2019, at 9:35 PM. A I am opening my eyes I instantly see an image to my right of multiple lines entangled together with static electricity intertwined within the lines. The tangled lines reminded me of what we called Jack Frost on windowpanes as kids. The observation lasted about fifteen seconds and slowly faded. I did not feel anything nudge or push me, so I am not sure why I woke up.

Sunday November 3rd, 2019, Karen was nudged twice that startled her to a wake. She opened her eyes and scanned the room briefly, sat up, looked around, and confirmed nobody was in the room with her, noting nothing else seemed unusual or out of place. I asked her what time this happened, she replied with, "I never thought to look at the clock."

Monday November 4th, 2019, at 8:21 PM. While reading in my chair, a group of primary lines, with a secondary line moving very slightly around the primary lines, appeared three feet in front of me. Karen is around the corner in the bathroom, I call out for her to come out here to see these lines, they are exceptionally clear, but as she enters the room, they immediately disappear, and she does not see anything.

Tuesday November 5th, 2019, at 11:10 PM. While I am reading on my cell phone in the recliner with the nightlight on, something unknown but intuitive provokes me to look up and see two straight vertical lines about two feet in long. These vertical lines serve as primary lines that are noticeably clear and visible, each with a separate secondary line that pulsates a bright, yellow orange color. Towards the top of both primary vertical it looks like the shape is starting to change, but it does not happen, and slowly fades away.

Tuesday November 12th, 2019, at 2:40 PM. I open my eyes and look around, nothing visible caused me to wake, so I quickly fall back to sleep. I feel a nudge on my knee that wakes me up to notice right away it is 2:40 AM. I look up to see four primary vertical lines; each line has a separate secondary line of movement. Without any hesitation, I loudly say, "Hi, it's good to see you again!" Now I am getting drowsy and falling asleep. How long the lines were there I do not know, I become drowsy watching them and fall asleep…

Monday November 18th, 2019, at 2:30 AM. As I rise from the recliner in my bedroom, I notice the nightlight next to me suddenly became brighter and catches my attention. I observe briefly as the nightlight continues to grow brighter. I walked down the hall to make a comparison to that nightlight, and observed it was glowing at a normal and unchanging brightness. I went to the bathroom nightlight to compare; the light is glowing like that on the one in the hallway. I return right away to the bedroom to see the nightlight glowing normal again.

Wednesday November 20th, 2019, at 7:40 PM. As I am walking from the living room into the bedroom; I see three primary lines slightly to my right, about six feet from the floor. As before, the primary lines each have a separate, secondary, line of pulsating energy from top to bottom. I watch them until they quickly fade away.

Sunday November 24th, 2019, at 8:40 PM. I awaken to see; one primary, horizontal line to my left with a separate secondary line of pulsating energy moving clearly along the primary horizontal line until slowly fading. Next, I observe a primary vertical line directly in front of me (about 6 feet away) with a clear separate secondary line of energy moving along the primary lines in a pulsating motion until it fades away. I wonder if this is the same line observed twice in separate directions?

Saturday November 30th, 2019, at 11:38 PM. As I woke up, I noticed two bright reflections moving around the fuse box in the kitchen. I paused to watch, and eventually I realized they were; two, bright white orbs about the size of baseballs, moving in a figure eight pattern, two feet from the ceiling. I observe for twenty seconds until they disappear only to reappear fifteen short minutes later! I pause to watch the activity that has returned to the room for about twenty seconds until they disappear. Another fifteen minutes pass when I witness for a third time the same bright white orbs until they disappear twenty seconds later.

Wednesday December 11th, 2019, at 9:35 PM. My eyes open to a new experience. There is a mist that hangs loosely and hovering unrestricted in the air about a foot away from my face. I observe for only a few seconds before I watch the loose mist gather itself up midair to form a clear vertical rectangle. The rectangle is subdivided equally into four square sections that I can clearly see through. I knew that Karen was up and watching TV, so I called out for her to come in here! She enters the room saying, "what did you say?" but the image had already disappeared. I did not observe any color or pulsating energy.

Saturday December 14th, 2019, at 8:30 PM. I open my eyes to the feeling of a firm nudge on my knee, but do not see anything when I scan the room, so I fall back to sleep. I woke up a second time, although not from a nudge, I scanned the room and saw two dark, vertical lines with small dashes of color missing along the lines. The pair of vertical lines are encircled by a single stationary line have twisting around it like a rope then disappears.

Monday December 23rd, 2019, at 10:05 PM. As I read with the nightlight on, I am distracted by a nudge on my right knee. I look up from my book and immediately see a vertical curved line in front of me. The line instantly begins to pulsate and disappears in an instant.

Friday December 27th, 2019, at 9:40 PM. I feel asleep with the blankets over me. I woke up feeling some pressure on my leg and opened my eyes to see a group of solid lines; three feet directly in front me, moving extremely fast in a circular motion. I observe the activity for about thirty seconds before I fall back to sleep. I am comfortable observing these lines, so I close my eyes and fall back to sleep with the blanket over me.

Later that night, I woke to something pressing on my leg. I open my eyes and see the exact group of solid lines moving fast and circular. The observation lasts about thirty seconds and then suddenly vanishes, as if I turned the light switch off.

Volume Two

Chapter 6

A Very Active Year

2020

January 14th, 2020, at 5:30 PM. I am relaxing in the front room watching TV with the front room light on. Karen is walking out of the bedroom and down the hall towards me in the living room when she hears an unusually deep voice. Simultaneously, I hear the voice (but it does not sound deep to me). I am thinking she is saying something to me, so I call out turning back towards the bathroom, "I did not understand you." She replies as she is walking into the front room, "I thought you were saying something to me." We both heard the voice at the same time, no more than a few words were audible, and nothing was discernable.

Later that evening at 9:30 PM, I am in the bedroom thinking of the daily events we both experienced. Suddenly, there are two quick flashes, first to my left, and then to my right. I follow them abruptly turning my head from the then right side. Both flashes were the same color of bright orange, and yellowish.

January 15th, 2020, at 3:30 PM. I am lying in the recliner in the spare bedroom, (my sleeping and computer room) reading on my cell phone with the table lamp on next to me as I often do. A shadow passes through the nightlight creating a quick dimness in the room that I recognize. I can confirm quickly and easily by sight the lighting changes in the room.

The second event was on the same day at 4:00 PM. I was not completely asleep in the recliner when I woke startled from being hit on my left knee. I immediately put the recliner into the sitting position, and started looking around the room, but did not see anything that may have hit me, I was alone in the room.

January 16th, 2020, at 9:50 PM. I am sleeping in the recliner with the nightlight on when something firmly pressing on my knee wakes me up. As I open my eyes, I easily see a few short lines about six feet in front of me. Each short line has a sperate and secondary line that is clearer and more prominent compared to the short primary lines and is pulsating and flashing at a high rate of speed before slowly fading away.

January 22nd, 2020, at 6:45 PM. Karen is in the main bedroom when she heard an indiscernible deep male voice that she knew immediately was not mine. She can hear the voice down the hall between the room she is in and the room I am in. Simultaneously, I am on my recliner in the living room, and I can clearly hear the voice, but dismissed it as the TV. We both heard the voice at the same time, no more than a few words were audible, and nothing was

discernable.

January 27th, 2020, at 8:25 PM. I was asleep for about an hour under the blankets when I woke up and clearly saw one square three feet in front of me. The square is filled with a stationary milky cloud or foggy energy that is different than the parameter of the square. Even though the energy in the center is not clear, it remains transparent enough that I can see through the center. Loudly, I call for Karen to see this, expecting the square to fade and disappear as before when I call Karen. This time, the square remained stationary as Karen enters, "what are you seeing?" I pointed to the square, she replies, "Bill, I don't see anything." Expectedly, I begin to describe what I see, sharing that square has not yet moved. Karen still cannot see it, so she leaves the room.

Now, I slowly take my hands out from underneath the blanket, one at a time and reach for my cell phone to try and document this experience.

I also want to know if the square's source is interference from the wall nightlight, or something else, and confirm immediately it is not. I maintain my gaze on the square as it slowly moves over my legs to hover over me while I remain still under the blanket. I very slowly stretch out both of my arms to hold my hands underneath the square for about fifteen seconds before I start to lift my hand upwards towards the square as it remains stationary. I am shocked to observe the square moving upwards coordinated with me as I lift my hand further upwards. We slowly moved towards the ceiling in unison about one inch before Karen yells, "Bill, is it still there, can you see it?" I yell back, "yes!" as it starts to fade and move away from me, she replies, "wow!" and rushes into the room just as the square has completely faded to gone. How did these affect society's beliefs regarding sports?

January 30th, 2020, at 5:20 PM. Sleeping in the recliner I feel something firmly pushing down on my leg. I am waking up and opening my eyes, I can see a shadowy figure moving away from me. It is moving fast towards the window. The blinds at the window are closed, no light coming in or out of the window area. There was some light with the TV on, the only other light was the nightlight. The shadow is moving rapidly towards the window, going through the shades and the window.

January 31st, 2020, at 6:30 PM. Something touching my leg wakes me up. I fell asleep in the living room with the TV and nightlight on. I look around the room, I do not see anything. I get up and go into the small bedroom, watch TV while using the computer. Still being tired I get in my pajamas and then fall asleep in the recliner.

Second event this evening at 7:40 PM. I again wake to feel my leg being nudges hard enough to wake me startled. I do not see anything unusual. This has now happened several times, on the same day. I think to myself, I am getting used to these events. I cover myself up curious and wondering how I might communicate with this energy and easily fall asleep.

February 14th, 2020, at 8:40 PM. As I walk three to four feet from the spare bedroom to the bathroom when I see a dark outline of something that resembles a mannequin wearing a dark cloak. I stop walking forward to stare at the figure to become familiar with the shape. After about five seconds, it slowly fades. This was the first time I had seen anything like this.

February 18th, 2020, at 2:10 AM. Karen is asleep in her bed when she awakens to a very firm grip on her feet. She immediately sits up, looks around the room, but does not see anything unusual. She tells me that it felt as if a hand was grabbing both her feet at the same time.

February 19th, 2020, at 11:35 PM. I fall asleep in the front room in the recliner and spontaneously wake up to an image just above the couch and to my left. I notice that the image is made of dark, stationary lines to create a rectangle. Within the rectangle is what looks like only the body of a painted Eastern Dragon without a visible head, scales, or feet. I stare to identify the missing pieces of the dragon before it fades away.

February 24th, 2020, at 8:30 PM. I wake up with my head still turned to the right on the pillow (without being nudged that I notice). I lift my head and turn to the left to see two dark black lines moving in two different directions, one line vibrates off to the left and one line vibrates off to the right. The energy lines are only two feet in front of me so I can see their movements easily and clearly. One line continues to move towards the wall by the couch and actively passes through the furniture without any resistance and disappears into the wall. I did not see the second line disappear. I witness in awe for twenty seconds. Only seconds after I observed the lines disappear, I could hear three or four light taps coming from that exact spot on the wall.

Observing lines and movement in different forms has become a regular occurrence for me. I spend some time reflecting in my recliner on my many past paranormal experiences. I ponder how and why these events occur. I know for certain; I want these events to continue. Easily, I return to sleep.

March 19th, 2020, at 10:08 PM. The usual firm nudge on my leg wakes me. I look up, to the left, and three feet below the ceiling, to see a group of circles. The circles are transparent and stacked vertically, touching along sections of their perimeter, and moving in an upwards direction familiar to an escalator. I watch for about twenty seconds before they slowly fade away.

March 22nd, 2020, at 2:10 AM. I wake without being provoked to see a dark square; suspended in midair, five feet in front of me, and six feet from up from the floor. The square slowly moves until it is straight above me while I lay still in the recliner. I scream out with surprise as I watch it travel through the wall to disappear.

April 14th, 2020, at 1:30 AM. I fell asleep in my recliner in the living room, as usual. Behind me on the table is my lamp that I had turned off before I fell asleep. I wake naturally and open my eyes to see an image; midair, and five feet away, made of dark lines that remind me of a long and slender belt (one inch wide by three feet long). I calmly watch the image slowly start to float upwards and towards me. Simultaneously, the stubs of hair move by what feels familiar to a light touch. I raise my arm to reach for the image, but as I move my fingers to touch it, I instead watch my fingers swing through the image without any resistance or connection to a solid object. I reach back towards the lamp, my gaze follows, to turn on the light. My gaze returned immediately to the image, but it was gone, nothing was there! I have noticed from previous experiences that images will often disappear immediately when the light turns on.

April 26th, 2020, at; 2:14 AM., 2:30 AM., and 3:00 AM. I observed three identical events this morning.

First event (2:14 AM). I wake up naturally in my recliner and notice off to my left an image of three squares connected and overlapping only at the corners. When facing the squares, the middle square hangs lower than the square on right and left. I also noticed that each square holds a different shade of gray.

The Second and Third events (2:30 AM and 3:00) AM; everything I experienced during the first event was experienced identically during the second and third event, apart from the location that the squares presented themselves in the room. The second set of squares was presented in the center of the room, directly in front of me, and the third set of squares was presented to the right of me. I did not observe any change in color and size.

I observe each event for no more than a minute before I naturally fall back to sleep, uninterested and unbothered. I never reached for the light, my glasses, or my phone.

April 29th, 2020, at 3:15 AM. I am nudged on my leg and open my eyes to see an image only two inches away from my face, so I yell out in surprise. I see several green and yellow-orange vertical lines moving very slightly and curved at each end. I stop in my tracks so that my nose does not hit it and observe in silence for about fifteen or twenty seconds. The lines remain to my left moving very slowly and seemingly unaware of me, so I stretch out my fingertips to touch the lines, but my fingers go through it. The lines stop moving as I wave my fingers around to confirm I do not feel anything; solid, cold, or hot. I pull my fingers away as it fades rapidly. I move forward with my morning.

April 30th, 2020, at 1:30 AM. I wake up and head to the kitchen for coffee. As I enter the room, something in front of me and to my left catches my eye and I immediately recognize the exact lines from yesterday morning. Since I have already been stopped in my tracks and the lines remarkably close to my face, I say very softly, clearly, and directly, "you were here yesterday morning." I already have my glasses on, so I am positive these are the lines I have seen several times before. I reach out to lightly touch the lines with only a few fingers to confirm if the lines are solid. Both the Lines and I remain still as I withdraw my hand away from lines and immediately cover my left eye with my left hand to see if I am hallucinating and to check my overall visual field. No change as I continue to see the Lines very clearly. I immediately do the same with my right eye in which I confirm the lines remain visible, still, and overall unchanged. Great, both eyes are still working correctly, so I say, "What would you like to talk about?" My voice provokes the lines to begin to significantly dim and move backwards and away from me. I hold my gaze as the lines move down the hallway towards the bathroom until the lines fully fade to gone in a matter of seconds.

The lines did not see it fade or disappear, just gone, like a light switch. I continue to feel confident that this visit was the same set of lines from previous nights around the same time. Random visits from lines are becoming normalized for me.

May 1st, 2020, at 3:20 AM. I wake up naturally in my recliner, and without a nudge, to see lines in a new pattern extraordinarily close to my face. There are five lines mid-air arranged in neat parallels. The lines appear thicker than what I am used to seeing, and brighter. The first, third, and fifth lines are solid while the second, and fourth, are segmented and remarkably clear (the 'visiting lines' are arranged just like the lines on a two-way street). I outstretch my arm and hand to try and make physical contact. Gradually, my fingers reach the bottom of the lines and eventually my entire hand is behind the lines. I can see my hand clearly while I simultaneously clearly see the lines in front of my hand. I continue to hold my hand still behind the lines and gingerly begin moving only my eyes; right, left then up, and down. The object does not move! I maintain my gaze on the lines and very slowly begin to turn my whole head to the right and then to the left. I am getting excited because my movements do not provoke the lines to disappear. In that moment, I perceived the stillness of the lines as an attempt at communication from the lines to me or the lines have become comfortable in my presence.

Next, I notice my cell phone lights up very brightly and then begins to restart. The light from the phone restarting pulls my head and attention while I hold my hand still and keep my arm stretched (I am trying to avoid intentionally making any sudden movements). I am thinking there must have been an auto update on the phone (weird timing). My gaze returns to the lines, but they are gone. I am left sitting in the recliner by myself with my arms outstretched. The lines disappeared as I turned my head.

Movement of any kind is the cause of an event to end or lines to disappear. I reflect and wonder if this will be the longest episode of lines I will ever see and try to touch. Regardless, I am excited by this encounter.

May 11th, 2020, at 1:20 AM. And 3:35 AM. I am reclining in my chair quietly listening to programs on the radio with just the nightlight on when a sudden movement from my left peripheral vision steals away my attention. As my head turns to the left, I immediately see the same group of five lines from the night before! The five lines are midair and at eye level and remarkably close, about a foot away from my face, although not as clear compared with May 1st's visit. I put my glasses on expecting to see the lines clearer, but there was no change. I cover the left eye with my hand, no visible change. I do the same with my right eye while I simultaneously move my head to the right. I feel amazed to notice the lines are following my movement! I remove my hand but not the position of my head as I observe the stationary lines for only a few moments before they fade away. I thought this event was interesting, so I wrote it down and fell back asleep.

Second Event at 3:35 AM. I am still asleep from my past encounter when I am awakened by a nudge at 3:35 (my head tilted toward the alarm clock so I could easily see the time). My eyes automatically turn to the right to see my five lines are back. The lines seem friendly, and I trust them, so I reach out to sneak a touch, but they move backwards and quickly disappear. I am disappointed the lines did not stay a bit the way they did two hours earlier. Regardless, I easily fall back to sleep.

My interests and beliefs in the paranormal are growing as I continue to ask questions and seek answers.

May 12th, 2020, at 12:45 AM. and 3:30 AM. I was awake but with my eyes closed listening to the radio. I randomly open my eyes (no nudge or push) to see directly in front of me in midair are my very friendly lines. I decide not to try reaching out and instead I say, "I am happy seeing you tonight." I glance at my radio to confirm the time then reach for my glasses expecting the lines to disappear while my eyes are diverted. With my glasses now on I return my gaze to the five lines. They stay in place, so I changed my response to their presence, and I deliberately ignored them hoping for some type of new reaction from the lines. My eyes look down at my cell phone for about fifteen seconds before I glance back up at the image. The lines have relocated to my left side. I returned my attention to my phone to read for a while.

Later, I checked back in at the clock confirming almost twenty minutes had passed without the lines leaving my left side or disappearing altogether. I feel compelled to say something to the lines about how long they have been here with me. As my head lifts from the clock the lines are gone, I waited too long to say something. I am upset with myself; however, I quickly fall back to sleep with the radio on.

Second Event at 3:30 AM. I woke up with the ear bud still in my ear and noticed the time was 3:30 AM. I stopped the radio, removed the ear bud, and glanced up to see the same set of five lines. I say, "I thought you did not want to see me anymore." I immediately fell back asleep after saying it. Even if I wanted to stay awake, I did not have any control to stay awake. Something wakes me back up and I immediately check the clock and notice ten minutes have passed. Next, I look straight ahead to see two images. One is rectangular and floating midair in a vertical position. The second image is large, circular and reminds me of a globe of the Earth. I can see through the circular image to the other side of the room, and I can also see something inside it that I cannot quite make out for sure. I spend a few quiet minutes looking and trying to analyze what they could be before they vanished in an instant like a light being turned off.

May 16th, 2020, at 5:30 PM. I get up from the chair after using the computer and see two streaks of very bright light that look like pair of slightly uneven equal signs (=) floating midair. Streak one is floating midair horizontally and sitting above and parallel to the second streak and measures around one foot in length by a half in in width and visibly brighter. Streak two is only a half foot in length, sitting about a foot underneath streak one, and otherwise identical. The streaks stay about five seconds then disappear.

May 17th, 2020, at 5:05 AM. I laid awake in bed for a while thinking about breakfast and making some morning coffee. Eventually, I toss the blanket off and immediately see something in front of me that is unclear and actively changing shape while in midair. The energy is floating like a cloud that dropped from the sky. I watch the fog slowly change from a random and unrestricted shape to equal signs (=), similarly to the visit from May 16th, except the lines are not solid, they are dashes, and equal in length. I watch the shape continue to take form as it begins slowly moving away from me before disappearing.

May 21st, 2020, at 3:00 PM. I am standing to watch TV in the front room when something off to my right catches the corner of my eye. I turn towards it and see what looks like a cloudy area has formed out of midair one yard away from me by the patio slider. The cloud is round but not perfectly round and puffy like a cumulus cloud but transparent. I watched it move upwards towards the ceiling until it was gone.

May 28th, 2020, at 10:30 PM. I am watching a little TV without the lights on when something to my left pulls my attention away. This visit appears as four solid lines each about one foot long floating vertically in midair and evenly spaced one inch apart from each other. I watch the lines begin moving closer to me until they seem to stop intentionally about one foot from my face. I reach out to touch the lines since I am so close, but my fingers pass through the lines without feeling anything or changing their shape. As I pull my hand back, the lines change from a vertical to a horizontal position, then revert to a vertical position. The lines pause their movement as a new line begins to encase the vertical lines in a square shape. The lines remain inside the new square line but begin to morph into an odd shape inside the square and pulsate while the new line forming the square remains stationary. I am getting extremely excited about what is happening so I loudly yell, "Karen, Karen, you have got to come see these lines!" I continued calling Karen, but the paranormal lines quickly faded away before she entered the room. I told her later I had a sense of de ja vu right away with these lines! We were both wowed and amazed!

June 9th, 2020, at 3:35 AM. I wake up to a small group of flashing lines to my right. I assume the lines woke me up. I say, "good morning, how are you?" My voice provokes the lines to move slowly towards me and I sense they are deliberately moving slowly not to frighten me. They stop short one inch from my face (it is unbelievable being they are so close). I reached for my glasses, slow and steady, and put them on, while the group of lines remained stationary. I blinked my eye a couple times to make sure there was no debris distorting my vision, both were clear. The lines begin moving backwards as I gasp with astonishment and plead, "do not go!" stopping about six inches from my face. The lines start moving backwards and sideways for no apparent reason, so I reposition my head to try and see them from a new angle. I only notice their shapes are irregular with no definite outline. The lines make it about five or six feet from me before quickly disappearing out of sight but not out of mind.

June 13th, 2020, at 10:35 PM. I wake from sleep spontaneously and see to my right a group of small and tightly grouped circles floating midair in front of me. I notice each circle is made of a dark and opaque primary line. Each circle has a separate and secondary line that pulsates and moves circular around each individual circle. This group of circles does not stay long before they rapidly move upwards and to the left before disappearing out of sight. I noticed this group of circles there were more than usual in quantity but overall smaller in size.

June 14th, 2020, at 3:20 AM. I spontaneously open my eyes from sleep and immediately notice friendly an orange-yellow orb close to my face, so close it could touch my eyelashes (but never does). I say, "do not go inside my eyes," as the orb floats up to the ceiling and through the ceiling without any hesitation. The orb seems friendly each time it visits.

August 5th, 2020, at 1:30 AM. My eyes open to an orange-yellow orb only an inch from my face and I jerk backwards in my recliner. Simultaneously, the orb begins to float backwards so I slowly reach out my hand to try and make contact, but the orb starts moving backwards too fast and fades before I touch it. Why is this happening again?

August 20th, 2020, at 10:35 PM., and 11:35 PM. I fell asleep on my right side and woke up startled by a firm push on my left knee that can be felt up to my left shoulder. As I open my eyes, I see two dark spirals made of circles that twist around each other at regular intervals and resemble an equal sign (=). The strands of circles are parallel resembling a barbwire fence without all the awful spikes. The equal signs quickly float upwards at a 45-degree angle towards the ceiling corner then out of sight.

Second event at 1:35 PM., I lay awake on my right side in my recliner when I feel a firm push on my left shoulder. I roll onto my left side expecting to see Karen and instead I am met with a cloudy area floating in midair that immediately travels upwards and through the ceiling with truly little time for observation.

August 20th, 2020, at 11:00 PM. Karen is in a twilight sleep on the bed in her room when she feels the mattress being depressed, like someone sat down at the corner toward the end of the bed. She sits upright to look around but does not see anything out of the ordinary.

August 21st, 2020, at 12:10 AM. About one hour later, she feels what is familiar to someone sitting down on the corner of the bed, but she never saw anything.

September 4th, 2020, at 6:25 PM. I awaken from sleep to what feels like my hand has been grabbed, reminding me of when Karen would grab my hand when we walk together. I scanned the room but did not see anything different in the room. I wondered if one of my paranormal visits was trying to hold my hand?

September 5th, 2020, at 4:30 AM. I wake up to a firm push on my left leg and I see something I do not recognize. I sit fully upright and meet a small square midair and only a few inches from my face. a kid building block, I stay quiet and stare to notice this small square has an opaque center and reminds me of a building block from my childhood. After a few seconds of observation, I begin blinking and rubbing both eyes, but the little square building block is still in the same spot. I cover each eye, one at a time, like prepping for an eye exam, but the square still does not move. I slowly start to change position to get up and as I do the square moves a few inches further away from me and slowly fades away until gone.

September 9th, 2020, at 7:45 PM. As I sit in the recliner listening to the radio in the dark, I feel a firm push on my right thigh. I turn on the light to inspect the room and notice a cloudy area hovering just above my leg. I hurriedly put my glasses on to clearly see this event more clearly and notice the cloudy area is irregular and semi-opaque. I watch it slowly move to my right and upwards towards the ceiling until I see it make contact and stop briefly before continuing through the ceiling.

October 31st, 2020, at 3:15 AM. I wake up and right away I see; two, separate and distinct clusters, of short, dark lines, floating in midair, without any visible restrictions and bonded in place by an opaque white energy. Both groups of lines are directly in front of me and inches away from my face, one cluster on my right and the second one on left side, (these lines woke me up?)

I realize that I cannot see through the spaces in between the irregular pattern of small lines because of the opaque energy, so I intentionally move my head from side to side to observe if the lines follow me, and they do with only a slight delay. I blink both eyes several times in disbelief, and to see if somehow there is something solid in my eye and scratching me, but I can clearly see out of both eyes. Next, I lift my hand and reach out to try and connect with one section of the small lines, but my hand passes through without impact to my hand or to the floating lines. I do the same with a different section of lines and still no response or impact or the shape. I intentionally wave my hand underneath and then behind the group of lines with my hand and I distinguish that I cannot see my hand through either section of lines. Nor do I disturb, disrupt, or distort the energy lines.

Like I have during preceding energy visits, I block the light (only the nightlight is on) in the room by covering my eyes one at a time with my hand, but that does not affect the lines. I am slowly moving my hand downward; I still see both. As I put my glasses on the lines stay in front of me while I move, unbothered. I noticed only five minutes had passed. I say, "If you are always here, why don't we talk?" I continue with, "Can you tell me where you came from, do you have names?" Just as I finished my question, the one to my right side moved backwards and faded away. The one to my left stays a bit longer before moving, just a little, before it quickly fades and disappears. I get up and examine the other side of the room only to see the usual and ordinary; furniture, pictures, and the nightlight. So, I returned to sleep as usual, also unbothered.

November 18th, 2020, at 7:45 PM. While I watch TV, I feel a tap in my knee that is familiar to a human. I look down at my knee and see a small square object surrounded by what looks like mist, fog, or cloud. The foggy mist moves around the stationery square until it floats upwards towards the ceiling. The light on my table is on so I can clearly observe the paranormal visit. I watch it float to the ceiling without stopping and disappear from my sight. I shrug and return to the TV.

December 14th, 2020, at 2:00 AM. I toss the blanket off as I hop out of the recliner and head to the kitchen for coffee, I notice an orb midair in the living room. As I stand it is about one foot in front of me, stationary and seems my friendly. It looks orange yellow in color and opaque. As I walk toward the kitchen, I start reaching for the orb to see if I can make physical contact with it. Just then it just vanishes, not fading, just gone as if it was turned off with a switch. I continued into the kitchen.

Chapter 7

Years 2021-2023

January 4th, 2021, at 8:30 PM. I left the TV and lamp on while I slept in my recliner, my foot grabbed familiar to a human. My eyes are startled open to see the face of my father from when he was young. His image was midair and a good eight feet away from me and remained stationary with a relaxed or natural expression across his face and noticeably clear facial features. He only visited a few seconds before he disappeared. My dad passed away June 29,1999 at age 79. This was the only visit from him since he passed away. I used this visit to remember that I was holding his hand as he took his last breath.

January 12th, 2021, at 2:05 AM. I could not sleep so I read articles on my cell phone. The light is on my table and the room is lit like usual. I get distracted by a noise from the kitchen that instantly reminds me of something plastic audibly dropping to the floor with several bounces. My first thoughts were; we have a mouse; something was pushed off the counter. I am curious to see what the sound was and head toward the kitchen. I flip on the ceiling light and inspect the counter tops but do not see anything unusual, so I begin to scan the floor. Then, I noticed a small yellow nozzle tip to something I cannot yet identify on the floor and in an upright position, which I thought was interesting. At this point I am in the center of the kitchen towards the dining room. I pick the tip up and look around questioning how this could have fallen and where did it fall from? It seems unlikely the tip was in the center of the room during the day while we were moving around in the kitchen, we would have stepped on it or at least seen it on the counter. If it was on the counter what pushed it off? How unusual! I feel tired so I turn the kitchen light off and get back into the recliner to fall asleep.

Later in the morning I ask and show Karen, "Do you know what this [nozzle tip] is?" Karen replies, "It is the nozzle tip to the spray can of cooking oil I use. The tip came off when I took the cap off the can, and I lost it right away. Where did you find it? I never heard it fall." Before I say anything, she continues with, "I must have lost the tip at least two months ago while I was standing in the pantry." Interestingly, the pantry is positioned at the other end of the kitchen, fifteen feet away from where I picked up the nozzle tip off the floor. We walk into the pantry to inspect the can she is using; the nozzle tip is on and is visibly different from the tip I found on the floor. Karen had already replaced the can since there was no sense in holding onto the can that could not be used. I told Karen the story of what I experienced while she slept. It was hard for her to believe, but I had the tip in my hand and continued to show her. Karen never mentioned she lost the nozzle tip from a can; I was completely unaware of this happening.

There was a full two-month difference from the time Karen lost the tip and when we would have seen it on the counter, stepped on it in the kitchen or found it while sweeping and mopping. Where the nozzle tip fell while Karen was in the pantry or how it randomly returned to the kitchen with a few bounces. We joked that the pantry acted as a door to another dimension and now the experience is just another mystery for my journal.

January 18th, 2021, at 2:00 AM. I wake to the unusual smell of smoke that is discernably different from a fire or cigarette. I sat for a while in my recliner immersed in the smell without any visible smoke in the room. After a while, I recognized the smell as a pipe, a very pleasant pipe. This pipe smell is detectable randomly throughout the day and night for the next two weeks. I wake throughout the day and night routinely so I could smell that very distinct pipe-smell daily. I stopped smelling the pipe for a period of a few days so I set out to check with our apartment neighbors if anyone could smell the pipe, had been smoking a pipe, or had a guest over smoking a pipe. I did not connect with anyone who answered yes, and I never smelled a pipe in the apartment again.

January 20th, 2021, at 2:10 AM. I fell asleep in the recliner and woke up to a nudge on both of my legs at the same time just above the knees. I open my eyes and see five dark horizontal lines stationary while floating in midair just above both of my feet. Each line is two feet long and about two inches wide and opaque. I did not observe any flashing lights or movement of any kind. I do not let more than a few seconds pass before I throw on my glasses and reach for my cell phone to take a picture. I cannot get the damn phone to turn on. In frustration, I continue to tap on the phone and engage the button on the side, but the phone remains stubbornly off. Finally, I tap the phone, it turns on, so I hurry to ready the camera for a picture, but the lines are gone by the time I have it together. I mumble to myself a little and turn on the TV to start my day.

January 31st, 2021, at 12:20 AM. I had fallen asleep with my radio, an earbud still secure in my ear and the light on the table next to me. As I wake, I jump right into reading the headline news. After reading for a short while I heard something to my left fall. My first thought was one of the three plastic clamps had fallen off the curtains. I intentionally inspect the curtains, and confirm the clamps are on and in place. As I was pulling the recliner into the upright position, I noticed a dental floss container on the floor. Weird. So, I return the floss to the opposite side of the table, so I do not bump it off, set up my recliner for sleep and easily go back to sleep. When I woke up around five in the morning, I noticed right away the floss was back on the floor in the same spot I had picked it up at 12:20 AM. Hmm.

Later that same evening at 8:45 PM. I woke from sleep from a nudge on my leg just above the knee. I open my eyes and see what resembles a pop can in midair and right in front of my face. The pop can was not visibly well defined and was transparent, no label like you might expect to see on a pop can, either. Unfortunately, I did not have time to get my glasses on and watch this image before it faded away. There is always next time.

February 11th, 2021, at 8:40 PM. After some reflection on these paranormal and unusual experiences, I decide to increase the number of nightlights from one to several throughout the apartment so I will see the paranormal visits more clearly. Now there are two in the living room, one in the kitchen, one in the dining room, and one in the bedroom. Afterwards, I set up to sleep in my recliner.

I am asleep in my recliner when my leg is nudged on my knee that suddenly wakes me with a jerk. In midair, about six feet in front of me, I see a paranormal face with a goatee that is unfamiliar to me. The face has a strong, dark, and clear outline, that remained stationary the entire visit. The goatee looks white and opaque and stands out juxtaposed to the rest of their facial features. The visits last only a couple seconds before fading away. My automatic comparison to this paranormal face was an Anglo-Saxon male from long ago British Colonial times.

March 24th, 2021, at 7:00 PM. I had fallen asleep for about half hour and woke to see straight ahead and in midair a paranormal visit in the form of lines that look just like a kite with a curved tail. The paranormal kite remained six feet in front of me, so I easily observed it. The kite was made of dark and solid stationary lines with a secondary pulsating line around the kite in a brilliant orangish-yellow. I watched the kite pulsate for a few minutes before it escaped through the ceiling. Afterwards, I wrote the experience down and turned on the TV.

March 26th, 2021, at 7:45 PM. I open my eyes to see the same paranormal kite from two evenings ago. Everything is the same; the distance, colors, stationary and pulsating lines of orange yellow, right down to the curved kite tail. I observe the kite midair for a brief five seconds before it slowly starts moving upwards and through the ceiling. I shrug to myself and jot it down...

March 28th, 2021, at 6:45 AM. Karen and I are up early this morning, so we are having our coffee in the front room while watching a little TV. We both heard an unusual noise but ignored it until we both heard the noise a second time and simultaneously said, "what was that?" I get up and begin moving slowly around the room flicking different pieces of furniture to try duplicating the noise. I flick the lamp, couch, tables, chairs, and we can tell the sound is different. I flicked every surface and texture I could find and eventually returned to where I started, and I was unable to duplicate the noise. Karen had been watching and suggests, "flick the wastepaper basket." Indeed, the sound is duplicated! I flick the wastepaper basket a couple more times for good measure and consistently create the matching sound. Something we could not see may have been hitting the wastepaper basket. I jot this event down with my next cup of coffee.

April 25th, 2021, at 7:45 and 9:00 PM, and 9 PM-3AM. I opened my eyes to a firm nudge against my knee, I felt like I was just hit, so I reached for my knee to rub it. I sit up in my recliner to look around the room, but I do not notice anything unusual. Since I am up, I make a quick run to the kitchen, return to my recliner, and then return quickly to sleep.

Second Event, 9 PM, I wake to a firm nudge against my knee. I scan the room for a paranormal visit of some kind, but I do not see anything. So, I fell back to sleep.

Third Event, 9PM (April25th) - 3AM (April 26th) Intermittently over the course of six hours, Karen observes me talking in my sleep repositioning with restlessness but remained in my recliner throughout the night. The next day, Karen tells me, "You were talking in your sleep on and off all night similar to a one-way conversation, not like a typical nightmare."

May 13th, 2021, at 8:10 PM. I open my eyes to a nudge on my left knee and see a paranormal visit floating just above the blanket. This paranormal visit presented as something familiar to a basic school ruler, but a little shorter, about five inches, and equally as flat. I got the feeling I was only seeing the second half of the ruler and that the first half had passed by me before I opened my eyes. I did not observe any flashing, waviness, nor did I notice any number increments along the edge like you would expect to see on an actual ruler. The ruler floated straight towards me supporting just a small distance above the blankets alternating between my right leg, then my left, until right above my abdomen where it veered off to the right and out of sight. I wrote this paranormal visit down and gave Karen an update the following day.

May 24th, 2021, at 10:20 PM. and 11:50 PM. I wake up and see a small group of circles that look like bubbles entwined and floating upwards towards the ceiling. I watch the circles for only a short while to notice they are not in any specific or recognizable shape or pattern and move slowly upwards towards the ceiling before fully disappearing. I fell back to sleep right away; I have seen the bubble before.

Second visit at 11:50 PM Later, I awaken naturally to see the same group of bubbly circles floating in midair. The circles are about the size of a softball, have a light transparent tan color with some visible texture I can quite identify. I watch the bubbly circles float gently and gracefully upwards and go through the ceiling. I know Karen will tell me to write this visit down.

July 22nd, 2021, at 8:45 PM. I wake and see something on the blanket and started frantically brushing it off me as it bolts away from me equally as frantic. This visitor was bigger than I am used to, I could feel the weight of the visitor in the bed with me even though I could not see an impression in the recliner. The next day I spent some personal quiet time, thought about this visitor, and wondered if it could have been the spirit of a cat or dog resting with me? I started to drought myself a little while

I was reflecting but I know what I saw. My eyes were open, I was not dreaming, I knew what I saw.

July 26th, 2021, at 9:30 PM. I fell asleep in the recliner with the table lamp on. I had slightly woken up and felt like something was moving along the length of my leg. The feeling starts as a slow movement and then rapidly travels down the outside of my leg along the outside of my pants and stops just above my knee. There, I see a milky cloud-like mist that remains stationary as it hovers above the knee while I try reaching for it. Just as expected, the mist dashes away from me to disappear in an instant.

July 28th, 2021, at 8:15 PM. The mist came to visit me again today and everything about the visit seems to be identical; the way I woke up, the appearance of the mist, where I noticed the mist hover above the knee right down the way the mist dashes away as it begins to dissipate. A very quick visit tonight and not much to write down.

July 29th, 2021, at 7:15 PM. This evening, I experienced the third consecutive visit from the mist. I woke up from the same movement moving down the outside of my leg. I expect the mist to be above my knee and I am not surprised to confirm it is there. I watch the mist as it moves slowly away from me until I lose sight of it about 10 feet away.

August 7th, 2021, at 7:50 PM. I yelp awake from sleep surprised by a firm nudge just above both of my knees. I frantically grabbed and pulled at my knees thinking something or someone was there. I did not see anything on the recliner or anywhere in the room. I know I expected to see either the lines, circles, or mist.

September 8th, 2021, at 6:50 PM and 7:50 PM. I fell asleep naturally in my recliner and awoke to the feeling of my leg being shaken and then the spot just above my knee was squeezed. I fell asleep, thirty minutes have passed. I slowly open my eyes, and I am startled that I do not see anything out of the ordinary. What I do see are the usual in the room; drapes are shut, nightlight on, (during this time of the evening I have ample daylight in the room), the air conditioner is not on, or the furnace fan, nor is the fan in my room. I stand up out of the recliner and continue to look around the room to see a small candle is lit and the flame is blowing wildly in a horizontal position. I stand still and silent to listen for the sound or feeling of the air whooshing through the air ducks, but I do not hear or feel anything. I decided to wait it out. I sat in my recliner two feet away from the candle watching this flame lay flat then alternating position to dancing with wild motion.

Second Event at 8:50 PM. I sleep for one hour in the recliner. I wake up to my right leg grabbed and followed by a firm shake. I look around the room and I do not see anything initially and then realize the candle is still lit with a normal upwards flame. I got up for a while and eventually wrote it all down.

October 12th, 2021, at 6:45 PM. The light is on while I quietly read the news. Out of the corner of my eye something catches my attention several times. I look up and around the room each time and I do not notice anything, so I return to the news. After a long while, I am tired and ready for my evening nap, so I turn off the kindle and as I reach for the table lamp, I see out of the corner of my eye I see a group of circles. The circles are intertwined and quickly rotate around each other while staying connected at various points along each circle. Each circle holds a pulsating energy that is visible and vibrant. The circles are still midair as I watch them pulsate for a good 15 seconds before speeding upwards through the ceiling, with purpose or fright. The performance was beautiful and unexpected. I assume these circles are connected to whatever was catching my attention during the news. I wrote it all down later in the week.

*October 28th, 2021, at 4:21 PM. I am wat*ching TV in the living room with the table lamp on when a white mist suddenly appears midair in front of me and begins to slowly float past me towards the dining room. Initially, the misty area does not have any recognizable shape to. As I continued to watch it turn down the hall as it appeared to morph into what resembled the outline of a human figure, so I got up to follow it. As I turn down the hallway, I see it is empty. I missed it disappearing as I turned the corner, I thought to myself. Out of curiosity I must get up and follow the visits that resemble humans. During the next two weeks a figure that starts as a mist will appear several times in and popping up in various locations. I should have written down my experience after each event. I do not listen to my kids when they say to write it down, I put it off.

November 22nd, 2021, at 8:20 PM. I woke from sleep as I felt a push on my right side and turned over to see a new paranormal visitor. This visit resembled a cutting board that is long, narrow, and flat. Along two sides there are flashing blue and red lights. It floats over abruptly to my right side then hastily over the chair I am sitting in to go through the wall. That thing was moving like the police officers! Paranormal police officers? Ha! Such a different visit from those in the past.

March 7th, 2022, at 7:45 PM. I fell asleep lying flat in the recliner until I woke up from a nudge on my leg. My eyes open to find myself underneath a new paranormal visitor that resembles the number eight, or the infinite symbol, but is lying flat, and is slowly floating upwards towards the ceiling. The outline is dark and pulsating with red and white colors and reminds me of lines you see on a voice recorder. I quietly watch it float away from me and through the ceiling.

March 13th, 2022, at 6:30 PM. I was reading until I became distracted by four vertical lines ten feet in front of me. There is dull but pulsating movement of blue and red color along each line. As I get up to try and make physical contact, all four lines rapidly move to my left side. I yell, "Wait!" and in the instant, they fade away. I am left standing by myself in the room. Karen turns the corner and finds me standing there by myself and I jump right into the story. She asks me to write it down.

March 17th, 2022, at 6:30 PM. I fell asleep in the recliner with a light blanket over me. I feel a firm grip on my left knee, that resembles a strong human hand, and then starts shaking my leg. My eye lids fly open to see a dark straight-line midair in front of me. I watch briefly as the line starts moving from my left side over to my right side. It pauses, like it suddenly realizes I am awake and watching it. Then at full speed shoots straight upward through the ceiling to disappear. This is the firmest that I have been touched or pushed. I think the visits must be a form of energy that is connected to the physical contact that the visitors first make with me. Physical contact seems intentional and purposeful, but why? I can see the visitors want to wake me up but what do they want from me?

May 6th, 2022, at 6:28 and 8:01PM. I wake in my recliner from a push on both of my knees and see a visitor in the form of a rectangular box divided into eight equal sections. Each section has a unique and distinctive outline while the center is transparent, except for one which is cloudy and partially opaque. I watch the visitor for thirty seconds before it vanishes in thin air. I fell back to sleep unbothered.

Second Visit, 8:01PM For the second time I feel the push on my knees waking me up. I see the same visitor in the form of a rectangular box in front of me. As soon as I turn the light on it disappears. There really is not anything else I can do so I turned the light off and fell asleep.

This paranormal activity continues and off for the next six hours; I get pushed awake; I see the rectangle until the light is turned on; and then disappears so I go back to sleep. I had a terrible night's sleep and had to stop for a nap the following day. I do not mind the visits, but I do not see how pestering me all night got anything accomplished.

May 21st, 2022, at 7:21 PM. and 9:15 PM. I was reading in the living room in my recliner with just the light on when randomly my leg is aggressively pushed, I mean with force. I nearly jumped up out of the recliner with shock but as I urgently scanned the room, I did not see anything around me. What was that? I called out to Karen while she was in her bedroom to give her an update.

Second Event 9:15 PM. I am reading in my recliner, minding my own business, when my bald head gets rudely slapped and scares the s*** out of me! I say aloud in absolute disbelief, "what in the hell is going on here?" I scanned the room and of course no one was there, not even Karen. I gave her an update over coffee the next morning.

May 24th, 2022, at 6:45 PM. And 7:45 PM. Twice tonight while I slept both of my legs were firmly grabbed. Both events startled me awake, and as I scanned the room, I saw nothing unusual.

June 21st, 2022, at 7:48 PM. I wake up surprised and confused to both of my legs being shook around and grabbed. As I am reaching for my legs to see what is going on and see a tanned orb in midair in front of me. It is translucent, I can see through it. I tried reaching for it, but it vanished when I moved like they often do. Another aggressive visit. I wrote it down.

July 25th, 2022, at 12:15 AM. I am resting in the recliner with my eyes closed when I start to hear a loud crackling coming from the wastepaper basket. I recognize the sound from the last paranormal visitor that was wrinkling the paper in the garbage can. As the sound continues, I look around the room, but I do not see anything. I glance at the clock, it is 12:15 AM, I need to write that down. Next, I start to look for what is causing the sound. There are no mice rummaging in the basket looking for food. This crackling continued for ten minutes before becoming silent. I waited and without any more crackling noise I decided to get up.

As I reach down towards the recliner lever to put my feet down and return to the sitting position when the end of the recliner starts violently shaking for five long seconds. I instantly grab the recliner lever and get back to the reclined position and say aloud, "what the hell are you?" I decide to get up and as I turn the light on, I do not see anything unusual. I looked behind the recliner and no electrical cord problems were found. Everything in the room is normal, including the wastepaper basket and it is empty. I even confirmed with USGS that there was no earthquake on this date or time.

August 3rd, 2022, at 7:20 PM. I was sleeping in my recliner when I randomly woke up to an orb in front of my face! Surprised, I jerked my head away trying to dodge the orb if it started coming at me, but it remained stationary, so I disarmed to watch. The orb is the size of a softball and cloudy white so I cannot see all the way through it. An unknown amount of time passes, I calmly stare back at the orb, not knowing what to do or if I should say something like I sometimes do. I know I do not want it to leave. Suddenly, and without any warning, the orb vanishes in thin air. I look around the room for a bit before heading to the living room to update Karen.

August 6th, 2022, at 7:00 – 7:45 PM. Three times within a forty-five-minute timespan this event occurs. Something pushes my leg several times and wakes me up. The first two times I was pushed I opened my eyes and scanned the room, but did not see any sign of a paranormal visitor nor was Karen in the room. However, with the third event, I opened my eyes to a familiar bright white orb floating midair directly in front of me, no more than two feet from my face. I look a little closer, and yes, I recognize this orb's puffy white cloud shape that I have seen many times before. The orb visits for only a minute or so before it moves quickly upwards through the ceiling to disappear. I went back to sleep assuming the orb was going to continue to visit me all night keeping me awake, but I slept through the night, unbothered.

August 17th, 2022, at 9:55 PM. I was sitting in my recliner watching TV when I felt a rude nudge at my lower leg. I scanned the room and did not see anything, so I got up to head to the kitchen as I was planning to get up anyway. I shuffle into the kitchen to see a paranormal visitor that is unfamiliar and looks like an antique and decretive wire fence. I abruptly stop and duck to avoid walking headfirst into the fence with my face. I paused as I realized the fence was not moving, so I reached for it and watched my fingers pass through the fence to the other side. My hand does not disrupt the shape or create any flashing or pulsating. Loudly and slowly, I say, "what-in-the hell-am-I-looking-at," as the fence simultaneously disappeared. I straightened myself back out and continued to the pantry wondering what in the hell that was supposed to be about. I put off writing it down.

September 10th, 2022, at 7:48 PM. I fell asleep in my recliner and feel a flick on my kneecap that wakes me up right away. I open my eyes to see what looks like a sheet of lined loose-leaf paper from a notebook floating in midair in front of me but not close. The paper has illegible writing on it, and I think that the message might be for me, so I say, "you need to come closer, I'm not able to read it." The paper responds by slowly inching closer. Simultaneously, I reach for my glasses to see the writing appears more as a wavy pattern. As I start extending my arm to grab the paper out of the air, it starts backing away from me towards the bedroom wall. I turned on the light just as the paper disappeared. Why would I turn on the light? I felt like I had to.

Later in the day, Karen and I were walking in the park and came across a pond. The surface of the pond water had small ripples from the wind, and I immediately recognized the ripple pattern as exactly what I saw on the paper earlier in the day. I of course jumped back into the story with Karen when I saw the rippling water. She asked me to write the experience down so we can keep track of everything that continues to happen.

November 18th, 2022, at 5:35 PM. I wake from the familiar push on my leg. This time, I see a group of six lines ten feet in front of me. I watch the lines briefly as they are still stationary. As I sit up and lean forward to get a better look when the group speeds upwards through the ceiling. These visits are becoming routine and expected at this point. I am getting more serious about writing everything down.

November 19th, 2022, at 6:30 PM. I fell asleep with my glasses and light on, and I wake up from a strong push on my leg. I open my eyes and see a cloudy mist floating backwards and away from me. The cloudy mist starts floating in front of the light making shadows form on the wall while the light in the room visibly dims. I lay quietly and watch the mist go upwards through the ceiling.

On to the next year...

Chapter 8

Years 2023-2024

January 28th, 2023, at 7:11 PM. I am reading my kindle in the recliner with the light on. I feel something familiar to a person trying to grab my leg and pull it to the side. I pulled my leg away and swore aloud. I scanned the room and did not see anything moving around. What? I wait a while and once I feel like I am not going to get messed with again, I fall back asleep. I told Kaen in the morning when we had coffee.

February 4th, 2023, at 6:40 I fell asleep in the recliner with just the nightlight on when I feel a rude push on my leg just below the knee. I open my eyes to see 3 dark vertical lines midair in front of me. Each line holds a light red pulsating energy just on top of the lines. I watched them briefly and spontaneously the lines started moving backwards and away from me, vanishing quickly. I stayed awake pondering what the lines are supposed to be and why I must get nudged awake when they show up?

February 9th, 2023, at 5:20 AM. I am in the recliner relaxing with just the usual night light on. I see a white mist appear across the room and travel over to the lamp covering the lamp shade and dimming the entire room. I can see the outline of the mist is just a little bit darker than the inside. I watch the mist hover over the lamp briefly then rise into the air. When the mist had completely removed itself from the shade it abruptly disappeared, brightening up the room as it was before the paranormal mist showed up. I look around and I do not see anything else going on, so I get up mumbling to myself to start the coffee.

March 23rd, at 8:10 PM., and 8:25 PM. Sleeping in the recline I awake from feeling something grab my ankle, opening my eyes glancing at my ankle, then the clock, it is 8:10, I go back to sleep.

At 8:25 I feel a firm push on my lower leg, open my eyes, only noticing the time without seeing anything

April 17th, 2023, at 1:50 PM. I have an afternoon visit today while napping. Feeling a touch on my leg I do not open my eyes I am ignoring the touch; I want to nap. It touches me again. This time it is firmer; I open my eyes when I see a misty area moving very slowly upwards toward the ceiling and going through the ceiling. I do not know if this misty image is what woke me, but it must have been the culprit.

April 28th, 2023, at 10:37 PM. I am listening to the radio and playing games on the cell phone. I am starting to feel a small amount of pressure below my knee. The pressure slowly increases. I reach for my knee knowing nothing will be there while I look out into the living room expecting to see a paranormal visitor. This time there is a single midair line that is dark and curved with visibly separate energy flowing circular around the line while flashing and pulsating bright and powerful. Then it disappears after a minute or so, like a switch turned off. I am unbothered as the visit was brief and peaceful, so I fell back to sleep.

May 12th, 2023, at 9:30 PM. As I am playing games on my cell phone, I get distracted by the sound of the bag in garbage can being rustled, and it lasts about five seconds. Out of the corner of my eye I see someone pass through to the kitchen from down the hall. I did not look up and assumed it was Karen since she had been in the bedroom down the hall watching TV. A brief time passed when I realized I had never heard of any activity from Karen in the kitchen nor had I seen Karen come out of the kitchen. I can still hear the TV on so she must have fallen asleep. I get up to ask if she was just in the kitchen and meet a white shadow in the familiar form of a person as they quickly move from the bedroom towards the kitchen and disappear into the pantry at the far end of the kitchen. "Karen, was that you in the kitchen about ten minutes ago? She replies, "I never went into the kitchen." She says, "now we are getting paranormal visitors on a regular basis." I explain to her about the person walking into the kitchen from the bedroom. I will write it down right away.

May 16th, 2023, at 10:30 PM. While Karen is watching TV in the bedroom she sees three black orbs. The orbs are the size of golf balls and moved rapidly past her face and continued at close range past her and to her right, disappearing through the wall. the room I am in and says," did they come through here, did you see anything"? I say no. Karen jumps right into explaining what had just happened. She did not hear buzzing, or any other noise associated with these orbs.

September 25th, 2023, at 9:05 PM. and September 25, at 9:13 PM. I wake up when both of my legs grabbed with an outside pressure applied. Something makes me turn immediately to my right to see a new paranormal visitor. The visiting energy is flat and resembles a pizza pan with a bluish tint. I accidentally fell back to sleep and woke up only six minutes later (I happened to glance at the clock, so I was able to confirm the six minutes of dozing). I was happy that the pizza pan did not leave the room! So, I say, "wow, you didn't leave!" I get up and approach it and do not get far when it moves backwards and fades slowly from my vision.

April 1st, 2024, at 12:30 AM. Playing games on my cell phone I notice the light in the room is beginning to fade. To my left I see from the bottom of the shade upwards a cloud shaped mist covering the shade. As the mist moves upwards over the lamp the room gets brighter. I used the K-11 EMF meter, it was showing a strong four-light reading. There was a lot of energy in the room. The reading on the meter was normal when I tried it thirty minutes later.

Summary

Activity has quieted in a noticeable way but continues. Awakening from being nudged is still happening but the orbs have not appeared. Heat sensations on my arms have not returned, but my flashing lines and colors still happen. Sometimes a quick movement will catch my eye, but not with an identifiable image. Why quiet intervals between events happen, I do not know. I want to thank you for reading about my experiences, hoping you enjoyed the journey. I have been thinking about what other Paranormal events will occur in the future, hoping new encounters continue to happen. Being 77 years old and the past 14 years has been amazing. Please do not be afraid of what you see, you are not alone, share your events with everyone while staying focused. I am still living in Mentor Ohio with my wife Karen, I can be contacted at baskfour04@gmail.com.

BILL SIMONE

Bill Simone

www.ingramcontent.com/pod-product-compliance
Lightning Source LLC
LaVergne TN
LVHW010802170825
818744LV00008B/143